Two ways extend before you. Many choose "the way of Cain" (Jude 11), which asserts human power and wisdom but leads down to death. James and Jude—the brothers of Jesus—ask, "Who is wise and understanding among you?" (James 3:13). Their letters reveal a different way, God's way, which leads to life (Jude 21). As you study their letters, remember that the flowers of human wisdom always fade and fall. But the garlands of God's grace never fade away (James 1:9–12).

TO THE DIRECTOR

This student folder contains nine study leaflets and the enrichment magazine. Remove the staples and distribute the leaflets as indicated in the leaders guide. This magazine should be distributed at the first session for use throughout the course.

Magazine written by Michael Eschelbach.
Charts by Edward Engelbrecht.
Edited by Edward Engelbrecht.

Study pages written by Milton Rudnick.
Edited by Earl Gaulke.

This publication may be available in Braille, in large print, or on cassette tape for the visually impaired. Please allow 8 to 12 weeks for delivery. Write to Lutheran Braille Workers, P.O. Box 5000, Yucaipa, CA 92399; call toll-free 1-800-925-6092; or visit the website: www.LBWinc.org.

Cover illustration by Russ Flint.
Graphic design by Karen Pauls.

Enrichment Magazine

IN THIS ISSUE ...

ABOUT-FACE!

Do you know anyone who has championed a cause he or she once tried to defeat? History has many examples of people who gave their lives for something they once tried to destroy. For example, a young rabbi named Saul thought God wanted him to destroy the Christian church. But then the Lord appeared to Saul on the road to Damascus (Acts 9:1–22). Saul came face-to-face with the resurrected Savior. Jesus convinced Saul of his sin and of God's saving grace. Saul changed his name to Paul and spent the rest of his life defending the Christian faith.

James and Jude are two more examples of people who did an "about face" in their life and thinking. Jesus once reminded His disciples that "no prophet is accepted in his hometown" (Luke 4:24). James and Jude, half brothers of Jesus, also found it impossible to believe that God had sent their older brother as the Messiah. What changed James and Jude from mockers to defenders of the Lord Jesus?

Opposing Faces

The Gospels do not tell us much about the biological family of Jesus. We do know that Jesus had brothers and sisters (Matthew 13:56). These were half brothers and sisters, since Joseph was their father but God was the father of Jesus. The Gospels also report that the physical family of Jesus did not believe in Him.

On one occasion, when Jesus was teaching in a house, His brothers and mother came to take Him home because they thought He was out of His mind (Mark 3:21–34). The Gospels show the spiritual separation between Jesus' family and Jesus by the fact that they stayed *outside* the house where Jesus was teaching. In response, Jesus emphasized that those in the house—those who did His will—were really His brothers and sisters and mother. John's Gospel tells us plainly that Jesus' brothers did not believe in Him and spoke sarcastically to Him (John 7:1–5).

Before condemning James and Jude remember that Jesus had broken some basic rules of ancient culture. By living as a rabbi, He distinguished Himself socially from His family. By leaving the family trade, He left His family obligations on the shoulders of His younger siblings. Also consider that in first-century Judaism the oldest son had certain privileges and responsibilities (inheritance and family leadership). After years of holding to His family role, Jesus suddenly left home, acted like a great teacher, and purported to work miracles. No wonder His family thought He had lost His mind!

Turning About-face

How did James and Jude go from unbelief to living as rabbis and writers of New Testament Epistles? Their letters reveal that they came face-to-face with the truth, just like the apostle Paul. James clearly condemns the evils of unbelief, greed, hypocrisy, and failure to obey the truth. Jude focuses on the problem of false teachers and people who do not give honor where it is due. These brothers condemn many of their own weaknesses. They teach so clearly about these sins because they faced their brother after His resurrection from the dead.

James and Jude had rejected the brother who made atonement for their rejection and all their sins. The rabbi they sought to drag home burst the bonds of sin, death, and the devil. James and Jude thought Jesus was out of His mind, but it was the mind of Christ that knew how to save their lives. The wonder of Jesus' love and redemption turned their lives around. James and Jude became defenders of the faith they once ridiculed.

How are things in your family? No doubt, as in Jesus' family, you have experienced frustrations and disappointments. As you struggle to follow the Lord's teaching, be sure to set your family before Him. Pray for the heavenly Father to bless the members of your family and guide them in sincerity and truth.

Facing Jesus

When Jesus tells you to put the interests of others before your own, do you think He is out of His mind? Do you really turn the other cheek when someone does you wrong? Do you put some distance between yourself and Jesus when He says to seek His kingdom and righteousness first? We may easily assume we belong to the family of God because we regularly sit in His house, among His people. But if we refuse His instruction, then we prove that we are outside of His family. This is the truth of our human nature bound in pride and selfishness.

Your human nature is no different than that of James and Jude. Yet by the grace of God your spirit will be like theirs as well. You, too, can champion faith and love in the face of an unbelieving world!

Don't hide your face in your hands. By the grace of God, Jesus has come "outside" in order to draw you to Himself. Through God's Word the Holy Spirit creates a new spirit within you (Psalm 51:10; Jude 17–21). The reality of this new spirit is confirmed in your Baptism (John 3:3–6). This new spirit inspires faith and devotion. It confirms that you are a genuine member of the family of Christ (Jude 1). The Lord gives you strength and wisdom to silence your unbelieving human nature. The power of the Lord's resurrection continually turns you around to seek His grace and to share it with others. In His Word, see Him face-to-face. Reach out to others with His love. ■

No Pain, No Gain

After a football game, who has the most joy and satisfaction? You might argue that the player whose uniform is unsoiled and whose body does not ache would breathe a sigh of relief. However, a hot, dirty, aching player might convince you that he had the most fun. "No pain, no gain" he might say. This slogan points out that pain is a necessary part of improving strength and ability.

James expresses this reality when he tells you to "consider it pure joy ... whenever you face trials of many kinds" (1:2). Remember who you are and what is going on in your life. Jesus didn't call you to ride the bench. If you understand your time in this world as a serious contest, you will understand difficulty and pain as part of your progress in the faith. You can distinguish between trials and temptations.

Trials or Temptations?

There is an important difference between things that try our spirit and things that tempt our flesh. Knowing the difference enables us to appreciate trials and be strengthened by them. Such strength increases our ability to overcome temptation in joyful obedience to our Lord. How would your life be different if you considered every trial a joy?

James tells us plainly that God does not tempt anyone. Martin Luther repeats this truth in his explanation of the Sixth Petition of the Lord's Prayer. Luther writes, "God tempts no one ..." What is the difference, then, between God telling Abraham to sacrifice Isaac (Genesis 22) and Satan telling Jesus to jump off the temple (Matthew 4)? You will not find many outward differences between the events themselves. The difference is in the purpose or goal.

God's purpose in a trial is to increase our strength by testing it. Satan's purpose in temptation is to make us fail and fall from faith.

God, in His wisdom, uses Satan's activity for our benefit rather than harm (Genesis 50:19–21). The Holy Spirit was the One who led Jesus into the wilderness to be tempted. Satan was the one who actually did the tempting. Satan's purpose was to undermine and destroy the redeeming work of Jesus. God's purpose was to demonstrate His power over the devil.

Jesus resisted every temptation of the devil, and He did that on our behalf. He passed the test! He proved that He is Lord. Jesus demonstrated the potential of human nature filled with the Word of God. He also made clear the purpose of enduring trials and temptations. He endured all things so that we might live in His love.

What Are Temptations?

James explains that temptations are what our human nature feels (1:14–15). Human nature, separated from God by sin, lacks the fulfillment that God alone provides. Our human nature responds to this emptiness by trying to fill our lives with the only things available, things from the material world. The problem is that material things can never fill an infinite, spiritual need. So the temptation is to spend all our time gathering more possessions, even if this means disobeying God, hurting others, or abandoning our family.

Satan tempts us by continually appealing to our appetite for more. He shows us what we do not yet have. He leads us farther and farther from God. This is why James warns that we must not love the world or the things of the world (4:4).

If God Loves Me, Why Am I on Trial?

James says clearly that trials increase our strength as Christians, according to our spiritual nature (1:2–3). As an example, James refers to the testing that Job endured (5:11). James says that God is compassionate and merciful, but how is that true in the story of Job? Job did, in fact, have a strong faith in God. But the false thinking and words of Job's friends pushed Job to

God's purpose in a trial is to increase our strength by testing it.

Satan's purpose in temptation is to make us fail and fall from faith.

the breaking point. Job felt so attacked by his friends that he decided he needed to defend himself. Job's self-defense required him to call himself right and God wrong.

When Job finally reached the breaking point, God stepped in. God confronted Job for his words of self-defense and accusation. Job was horrified at his error but was quickly comforted by God's words of grace. After the trial Job's faith was even stronger than before.

God prepares us for growth when He shows us the weakness of our human nature. The apostle Paul once expressed this very truth as he confessed, "When I am weak, then I am strong" (2 Corinthians 12:10).

Passing the Test!

Athletic coaches have little patience for players who complain about the trials of training and competition. What can you do with an athlete who refuses to understand the consequences of the challenge in light of the larger goal? What can God do when people seek to protect their flesh at all costs while refusing to consider the more important life of their soul and spirit?

God's Law shows you clearly the folly of seeking to gratify your human nature in a material world that is passing away. What sense does it make to spend time indulging a human nature that is always turning away from the Lord of life? Protecting a body that is passing away at the expense of your soul makes no sense at all.

God is determined to see you through every trial and temptation in two ways. First, God has already endured every trial and temptation on your behalf in the person of Jesus Christ. The success of Christ is declared to you in the Gospel. Second, that very Gospel has also generated a spiritual nature in you that follows the pattern of your Redeemer. You can see that temptations reveal the weakness and need of your human nature. You can see that the same situation is an opportunity for your faith to grow strong as you look to God for strength, comfort, and deliverance (James 1:12). He will not fail or disappoint you. ■

Wait Just a Minute!

No matter how high you rev, how loudly you honk, or how forcefully you complain, you can't rush a stoplight. Like so many things in life, it has its own sense of timing. You just have to wait.

Trials. Perseverance. Maturity. James reminds us that trials provide the testing of our faith and that such faith produces perseverance or patience (1:2–4). The original Greek word for *perseverance* means "to bear up under a burden or endure." The disastrous consequences of sin in our lives make plain our need for endurance based on faith. James summarizes the events of life with patience in the middle. The purpose of patience is to make us mature, complete, and lacking in nothing.

Don't Mind the Wait

The first thing James teaches us about patience or perseverance is where it comes from. Patience is the product of faith. If we consider the opposite of patience, impatience, the truth of James's instruction becomes obvious. Why are people impatient? People who are not convinced of the value of what they are doing quickly give up and take an easier path. James would suggest the reason they give up is a lack of faith produced by trials.

For example, if you want to drive to the store to shop for fun, heavy traffic may cause you to give up and go back home. However, if you were going to the pharmacy because a loved one needed a prescription, you would endure the traffic. That is patience. The trials we experience teach us conviction about what is important in our lives. Conviction makes us willing to endure patiently, knowing that our purpose is well worth the wait.

The second thing James teaches about patience is what it produces in us. The work of patience is to make us perfect and complete. How does patient endurance do this? If impatience is a product of wanting things that are not worthwhile, then it follows that impatient people have lives that lack what is most valuable. Faith, produced by testing, convinces us of what matters most. Christian faith centers on Christ, who is the Lord of life. He patiently endured all things so that He might redeem our lives. His endurance climaxed in His crucifixion with the words "It is finished!"

Christ is our refuge in times of testing. Testing provides opportunities to gain conviction regarding Christ's saving work. That saving work makes us complete or mature.

Wait for Me!

Test your life and learn whether the following applies to you.

- You want to do what others suggest is most important, but you get frustrated and give up.
- Giving up on things makes you disappointed because you think you will miss out on the things or activities other people enjoy.
- You miss the lessons in faith that God's Word wants to teach you about wisdom and faith.

Christian, imagine the patience Jesus exercised as He waited on the heavenly Father. His calloused hands gripped and moved His earthly father's tools as He waited for the heavenly Father to call Him to preach. Jesus would have patiently led His brothers in learning the tools of the family trade. He would have endured their misunderstanding, impatience, and even their ridicule. In all these ways, He grew in wisdom (Luke 2:52), prepared by the school of life and the Holy Spirit for His great mission.

Dear friend, at this very moment the Spirit of God is at work to help you see your life for what it is. If you sense that you are incomplete, listen to the Word of the Lord through James. Endurance comes from knowing what is worth waiting for. Jesus Christ lived, died, and rose again for you. He has promised to provide so abundantly for you that James could say, "Every good and perfect gift is from above" (1:17). Christ is the greatest gift, the reason and strength to be patient and endure. His purpose for your life is that you share His worth with others. ■

Faith Really Works

Before addressing the issue of genuine faith, James expresses a most important principle. James admonishes us to "humbly accept the word planted in you, which can save you" (1:21). According to James, we are saved by faith. That faith is worked in us by the power of God's grace in His inspired Word. The problem is, we have ears and eyes that deceive us.

When Ears Don't Work

James warns that we must be doers of the Word and not hearers only, lest we deceive ourselves. To hear the Word but not do what it says is like looking at yourself in a mirror and then forgetting what you saw (James 1:22–25). Faith produced by the Word provides a true reflection of us. We see ourselves for who we are, and we also see who God has prepared us to be in Christ.

When Eyes Don't See

Another test of genuine faith has to do with partiality. Partiality means we make an unnecessary or unfair distinction between people. James asks how a person of genuine faith can show favor to a wealthy person and despise a poor person (James 2:1–4).

Genuine faith insists that we see ourselves for who we are. The Law shows us our sin, our failures, our need for help. Seeing that need opens our heart, ears, and eyes to receive the fullness of Christ in the Gospel. We may have thought we were rich, but the Law showed us our poverty. In our poverty Christ came to us and presented to us His riches: all that the Law requires and the forgiveness of all debts. Hearing and knowing this means we see other people differently.

A Christian no longer looks at people with selfish interest. People of faith do not think first of what another person can or can't do for them. Those who look at the Word and remember what they have seen notice people according to their need. So James reminds his readers that it is the wealthy people who are making life harder for them, while the poor are eager to help (2:5–7).

Testing Our Eyes and Ears

A person who expresses faith without works cannot stand the test of God's Law. A genuine faith always bears the fruit of good works. James presents Abraham as an example of such genuine faith.

Abraham believed the promises of God. On the basis of that faith God considered Abraham to be a righteous man. Abraham's faith also bore fruit. His faith was not only in his mind, but also in his life and actions. Abraham believed the promises of God with such certainty that he obeyed when God told him to sacrifice his dear son Isaac. Hebrews 11:17–19 tells us not only that Abraham believed but also what he believed. Abraham was willing to sacrifice Isaac in obedience to God because he believed that God was able to raise Isaac from the dead.

God had already done the impossible by giving Isaac to Abraham. Abraham and Sarah could not possibly have a child, yet God gave them Isaac, according to His Word. Abraham believed this same God could surely preserve that life, even in the face of death. Abraham was not disappointed. God did preserve the life of Isaac by providing a lamb that would take Isaac's place (Genesis 22:7–8, 13).

God's ultimate fulfillment of His promise to provide a lamb of sacrifice was fulfilled in Jesus. The incarnation of the Son of God demonstrates that God is the author of life. The life, death, and resurrection of Jesus demonstrate that God preserves the life He gives. This is why faith works. Faith in Jesus does what Jesus did. Faith trusts God for our life and well-being so that we can freely and boldly obey God in the service of other people.

Many try to grow and prosper spiritually without having their faith properly grounded in God's Word. James shows that everything begins with the Word (James 1:18; 2:23).

God's Word → Heard → Believed → Lived

G.MYERS

Live by Faith

There are many people of faith in history, such as Abraham, Sarah, and James. All of them were able to do extraordinary things because they trusted God. Jesus was the author and perfecter of that faith (Hebrews 12:2). He is the Word of God in human form. He is the author of life and gave life wherever He went. All of His life was given in service to others, service that meant condemnation and death. But death could not consume the author of life (Hebrews 5:9), so Jesus rose from the dead. That fact is the inspiration of faith.

If you want to live, really live both now and forever, consider Jesus. He lived in the fullest sense of the word and shared that life with others, including you. He makes the same possible for you. This truth inspires faith that is active, as Jesus was. The life of Christ convinces us that life is realized when we give ourselves in service to others. We are all the more convinced of this service because we know that God provides for our life both now and forever. With your faith firmly planted in Jesus, you will be a tree that bears real fruit. As the product of God's activity in your life, this fruit will bear the test of time and eternity. ■

From Rags to Riches

Andrew Carnegie was one of the wealthiest men in American history. During his life he provided funds for a multitude of charitable organizations. He helped communities create libraries and even granted funds to churches for the purchase of pipe organs! Why would such a wealthy person feel compelled to give so much of that wealth away? Mr. Carnegie once wrote about rich people who hoarded their money, "The man who dies thus rich dies disgraced."

Not everyone agrees with Carnegie's perspective. In fact, people today seem more determined than ever to accumulate wealth and protect it. James turns popular thinking about wealth and poverty upside down. He does not flatter the rich; he warns them. He does not pity the poor; he encourages them. If you consider yourself wealthy, James will urge you to reconsider. If you think you are poor, James will also disagree. James argues that treating people differently because of their abundance or lack of material wealth is a serious mistake because God is the true source of every good and perfect gift (1:17).

You Ought to Boast

At the very beginning of his letter, James tells believers who are both poor and rich to boast (1:9–10)! This is shocking. We are used to wealthy people boasting about their wealth. But what do the poor have to boast about? The poor ought to boast in the fact that God has raised them up. In the Beatitudes (Matthew 5:3–12) Jesus said that the poor in spirit are blessed because God's kingdom belongs to them. A person who is poor knows what it is to be empty. A person who has been unable to change his or her circumstance knows what it is to be helpless. These truths in the mind of a person make room for the love of Christ. Christ healed those who could not heal themselves. He raised the dead. He gave the riches of eternal life to people who thought they had nothing except death to look forward to.

On the other hand, James tells the rich to boast in the fact that they have been brought low. Why would a rich person boast over the loss of his or her riches? James does not say that these people necessarily lost their material wealth. These rich people were brought low by the Law.

The Law issues condemnation that no amount of material wealth can overcome. Even wealthy people, who could protect themselves from earthly prosecution, will still grow old and die, since the wages of sin is death (Romans 6:23). Therefore, a wealthy person is blessed who has learned from the Law that wealth and personal ability cannot save. Finding this out now means that repentance and faith in Christ can be in place before death and judgment. The Law teaches that all the money in the world cannot buy clothing that will cover sins. When

The 2,509 libraries generously funded by Andrew Carnegie provide a wealth of learning and a world of smiles still today.

wealthy people realize that all their best works are as filthy rags (Isaiah 64:6), then they will see clearly that the righteousness of Christ is clearly the covering they need.

James returns to this subject near the end of his letter (5:1–6). He issues such severe warnings against the rich because he has seen the temptation that wealth presents. Human nature, left to itself, will surely cling to a world that is passing away and pass away with it.

Briefly reflect on your personal and congregational prayers. If requests about money and health were taken away, what would remain of your prayers? What might this say about your focus in life?

Wealth without Worries

Jesus once told a story in order to draw a contrast between riches and wealth (Luke 16:19–31). There was a rich man who had the best of everything every day. There was a poor man, named Lazarus, who was full of sores and longed to eat the crumbs that would fall from the rich man's table. Who would you choose to be like? Most of us would gladly be the rich man and happily avoid the poor. But Jesus tells the story with a twist. Lazarus could only long for and hope in a gracious God. The rich man had no such need and paid no attention to God. The rich man died without faith and found himself in the eternal torment of hell. Lazarus also died but was not disappointed. He was delivered and comforted by God. Would you make the same choices again, knowing the rest of the story?

God demonstrates the wealth of His love for us by patiently showing us the poverty of our riches. Material wealth cannot give us life or preserve our life eternally. God is gracious to teach us this so that we might cling to and treasure true riches. True riches are found in the Lord Jesus and His Word (James 4:10). Here we find life and restoration, now and forever. In Christ we find purpose for our life, even our material goods and blessings. As God provides for us, we provide for others. If you are blessed with material wealth, you know how to use it in service to the Lord. But no matter what your material wealth, you are urged to grasp the real riches of faith and life eternal in Christ (James 4:11). ■

BROTHERS IN MINISTRY

This chart chronicles what the Bible teaches us about James and Jude, the brothers of Jesus. As you read about these brothers and their service in the church, consider the state of your family and your working relationships. Pray for joyful and peaceful service.

EVENTS

OVERVIEW

A sincere Jewish family
Mark 3:21–34
c. A.D. 27 or 28

We first hear about James and Jude because of their opposition to Jesus' teaching ministry in Galilee. The criticism spoken by Jesus' family mingled with the accusations of the teachers from Jerusalem, who asserted that Jesus was demon possessed. The family seems to have conscientiously followed the customs of first-century Judaism and respected such teachers of the law based in Jerusalem (see Luke 2:21–24, 39, 41–42). They probably regarded Jesus' appointing of disciples and His surprising teachings as a rebellion against religious authority. When they tried to "take charge" of Jesus (Mark 3:21), they may have sought to protect Him from the authorities (see Mark 3:6).

Application for you

Joseph and Mary did their best to raise their family. Yet this did not prevent them from experiencing conflict. The same is true for your family. So much of who you are depends on what you have learned and experienced in your family or nurturing relationships. Learn from the Lord's Word and do your best for your family. When you make mistakes, forgive yourself and also lead your children to sincere faith (James 1:16–18).

Sons of a carpenter
Matthew 13:55; Mark 6:3
c. A.D. 27 or 28

We next hear about James and Jude (Judas) from the lips of their neighbors in Nazareth. They describe the ordinary character of the family, uneducated descendants of a carpenter. "Carpenter" (*techton*) could mean a wood craftsman, a stonemason, or a metalworker. In the Gospels, Jesus frequently refers to stonework (Matthew 7:24–27; 16:18; 21:42–44; 24:1–2), perhaps indicating that the family trade was in stone construction instead of woodwork.

Application for you

Whether you stem from peasants or kings, God has purpose for your life (James 2:1–5; 4:13–17). Whatever the Lord gives you to do, do it with all your might.

EVENTS

OVERVIEW

Family jealousy
John 7:1–5
c. A.D. 29

The sarcasm of Jesus' brothers reveals jealousy and resentment over His popularity. It may also express fear, because Jesus was endangering Himself and His family. Jesus did not attend the Feast of Tabernacles with His family that year but went up to Jerusalem secretly with His disciples.

Application for you

When angry words divide your family, don't give up hope. Jesus knows the pain of such divisions. Seek your healing in His life-giving Words of peace (James 1:19–21).

Witness of the resurrection
1 Corinthians 15:7
c. A.D. 30

According to St. Paul, James was one of the first people Jesus appeared to after His resurrection. Jude does not seem to have held the same leadership role that James held. Jude is rarely mentioned.

Application for you

If members of your family attain prominence or status, don't resent them (James 1:9–10). Thank God for their service and prayerfully support them.

Reconciled to Jesus before Pentecost
Acts 1:14
c. A.D. 30

After the resurrection, Jesus' mother and brothers waited in Jerusalem with the early believers (Luke 24:52–53; Acts 1:13). At this time Peter seems to have been the leader of the church.

Application for you

Jesus sought out His brothers and mother. Despite their earlier disputes, they were reconciled to one another. When disputes arise in your family, pray for reconciliation through Christ (James 3:17–18).

James meets Paul
Galatians 1:19
c. A.D. 38

About three years after Paul's conversion, he met James in Jerusalem. James would later become an important advocate for Paul in the dispute over the mission to the Gentiles.

Application for you

Recognize the importance of relationships for the work of the church (James 2:8–13). Reach out to one another with encouragement.

EVENTS

OVERVIEW

James leads in Jerusalem
Acts 12:17
c. A.D. 43

After Peter escaped from prison, he mentioned James distinctly from the other disciples, marking James's rise as a leader in the Jerusalem church. Note: The name *James* (*Jacob* in Hebrew) was popular for first-century Jewish people. Don't confuse James the brother of Jesus with the brother of John (Acts 12:2) or the son of Alphaeus (Matthew 10:3; Acts 1:13).

Application for you

Leaders will come and go in your congregation. Appreciate the strengths of each and forgive their weaknesses (James 3:1–2).

James's strict Jewish representatives
Galatians 2:1–12
c. A.D. 49

Paul described another visit to Jerusalem, where he met with James. James, Peter, and John—regarded as pillars of the church—welcomed Paul. They encouraged him to preach to the Gentiles and collect alms for the poor in Jerusalem. When James sent representatives to the Jewish/Gentile congregation in Antioch, the strict Jewish purity practices of the representatives divided the Antioch congregation. This sparked a confrontation between Peter and Paul. It also led to the first church council in Jerusalem.

Application for you

If you have not experienced division in your church, know with certainty that you will. Because of sin, members of every congregation harbor sinful attitudes. When a division arises, don't panic. Turn to Jesus for help (James 4:6–10). Base your decisions on God's Word and love for your brothers and sisters in Christ.

Jerusalem Council
Acts 15:1–20
c. A.D. 49

James accepted Peter's report about faith among the Gentiles. He also accepted Paul and Barnabas's report about the progress of the Gentile mission. These decisions by James were key events at the first Jerusalem council of the church. James's judgment seems to have been instrumental in ending the dispute about the practices of the Gentile mission.

Application for you

Understand your authority and role in the church as a voter or church leader. Exercise your calling for the good of the church and the support of God's mission (James 5:7–11).

Joy over the Gentile mission
Acts 21:18–26
c. A.D. 57

When Paul visited Jerusalem before his arrest, he made a presentation to James and the elders of the Jerusalem church about the progress of the mission to the Gentiles. They praised God for the conversion of the Gentiles and warned Paul that false reports were circulating in Jerusalem about his mission activities. They encouraged Paul to purify himself according to Jewish custom, in order to quiet his critics.

Application for you

Support and encourage other servants of the Word (James 5:13–16). When you hear about good things happening in another congregation, don't resent. Rejoice!

In their letters, James and Jude introduce themselves as brothers of Jesus (James 1:1; Jude 1). Though at first they resented Jesus' ministry, they came to trust Him and became faithful preachers of His Word. How difficult it must have been to acknowledge their brother as the Christ! Yet the Holy Spirit led them to this truth.

Through His death and resurrection, Jesus not only reconciled you to the heavenly Father, He also reconciled you to your fellow believers. He cherishes you as His dear child and calls you as a member of His beloved family, the church. ■

Like his older half brother, Jesus, James came to bear the marks of his faith and devotion on his body. According to the ancient church historian Hegesippus, the apostle James prayed so often at the temple in Jerusalem, his knees grew hard and calloused like a camel's. Hegesippus also tells us that James was thrown from the high point of the temple, stoned, and beaten to death with a club for testifying about Jesus (c. A.D. 62).

Ask. Please!

On December 11, 2001, the *Mayo Clinic Proceedings* published a report on prayer. The report was based on a study of patients with heart disease. Five people prayed for half of the study's 799 participants at least once a day. After six months, researchers found no significant differences between those who were prayed for and those who were not. According to the leaders of the study, prayer is not effective at all.

However, more factors are involved in prayer than the study considered. The study provided no information about the spiritual disposition of the patients or about those who prayed for them. The study also assumed that the only way to measure the effectiveness of prayer is if you obtain exactly what you are asking for within the material world. This article will take a closer look at what God's Word teaches about truly effective prayer.

God's Invitation

The Bible records many invitations to pray. For example, God invited King Ahaz to ask for a sign (Isaiah 7:10–11). Jesus said, "Ask and it will be given to you; seek and you will find; knock and the door will be opened to you" (Matthew 7:7). Paul commanded the Thessalonian Christians to "pray continually" (1 Thessalonians 5:17).

God's invitation for us to pray also comes with evidence of His genuine intent to respond. For example, Abraham's servant prayed for help in identifying the woman who would become Isaac's wife. Before the servant had finished his prayer, the Lord answered it (Genesis 24:15). Paul was excited to write to the Ephesian Christians that God does even more than we think to ask for (Ephesians 3:20). James also urges us on to prayer in three different sections of his epistle (1:5–6; 4:2–3; 5:13–18). Now that we are sure of God's desire for us to pray, what else do we need to know?

The Prayer of Faith

James is specific about how we should pray and about the kind of person who may expect their prayer to be answered. James says that a person lacking wisdom should ask for it, but that person must ask in faith (1:5–6). Later in the epistle James refers again to the "prayer offered in faith" (5:15) and to the "prayer of a righteous man" (5:16). The connection between these features is fundamental.

Jesus once told of two men who went up to the temple to pray (Luke 18:9–14). One man was a Pharisee who was righteous in his own eyes. He thanked God that he was not wicked like other people. The other man was a tax collector. He prayed that God would be merciful. Jesus tells us that the man who prayed for mercy went home justified (righteous before God) rather than the other. The answer to prayer was linked to God's righteousness and mercy.

Faith, worked in us by God's Word and Spirit, covers us with the righteousness of Christ. This faith also gives us conviction that God's will and ways are right, leading us to obedience. The prayer of a person made righteous by faith is motivated by that faith and seeks God's will. This is why such prayer is effective.

Prayer with Wisdom

At the very beginning of his letter, James urges us to pray for wisdom. Wisdom from God provides insight and perspective. Wisdom allows us to understand how God is working and how to benefit from what He is doing. Most people have heard that God makes all things work together for good to those who love Him (Romans 8:28). Few people actually recognize why or how these things are working together. If we have wisdom to know how God is working, then we can also know what to pray for in accordance with His will. We can avoid coveting and asking with the wrong motives (James 4:2–3), since wisdom from God allows us to distinguish between what we need and what we don't need.

What we need most is the forgiveness of sins. Therefore, James's final words about prayer focus on forgiveness (James 5:13–18).

Suffering has a way of stirring one's conscience. Many a sick person wonders what wrong he or she has done to deserve this suffering. Many conclude it is punishment from God. Sometimes a person knows very well that the situation is in fact a specific result from sin in his or her life. Sometimes, though, suffering has nothing to do with a person's own sin. In either case, God wants to provide restoration. Regarding someone who is sick, James urges that the elders be called, that confession be made, and that prayers be offered up to God, who will grant forgiveness. God may provide temporal healing. He will certainly provide eternal healing for those who pray in faith and thank Him for His mercy.

Request Granted!

The Mayo Clinic study that showed no evidence for the effectiveness of prayer should not surprise you. You may have had a similar experience or know someone who also thinks that prayer does not work. But James explains what kind of prayer is ineffective and why: "You do not have, because you do not ask God. When you ask, you do not receive, because you ask with wrong motives, that you may spend what you get on your pleasures" (James 4:2–3). God has no interest in answering requests that would only lead you further away from Him.

Before you conclude that God is not listening to you or answering your prayers, ask yourself, "Why am I asking for this?" or "Why would God grant my request?" Fallen human nature thinks of itself and its comfort. So people often ask for the desires of their human nature. But material things hold the potential of taking over our lives. Human nature will always be disappointed in a God who refuses to grant requests that do not promote real life.

What a blessing it is to know that God wants us to pray and will surely answer. God answers the prayer of faith, offered up by a person made righteous by faith. Faith and righteousness teach us what is needful and what is contrary to our life as a Christian. The prayer of faith is in agreement with the Word that inspired that faith.

Faith teaches you to recognize what is needful. Faith teaches you how to understand experiences of suffering in a world broken by sin. Your inability provides a reason to turn your attention to God's great ability. He has not failed and will not fail you. In the life, death, and resurrection of His Son, He has provided you with a life that endures all things. Recognizing this truth allows you to thank God in times of difficulty and to seek His wisdom and grace to thrive as His child. ■

TIM TEEBKEN/ARTVILLE

Slow to speak, slow to anger, and quick to listen.

That is what James teaches about taming the tongue (1:19). He encourages this for two reasons: (1) we are the firstfruits of God's creation and (2) mankind's wrath does not work the righteousness of God. As God's creation, we are to act wisely by listening carefully and responding with careful speech. As God's servants, we are to be of the greatest possible help to others.

Ready Ears

Listening carefully before speaking accomplishes godly goals in at least three ways.

First, listening carefully demonstrates that we care about the person speaking. This is very disarming to a person who would like to think of us as opponents. When we listen carefully and ask questions to clarify and learn more, the person speaking will consider that we are not acting like an opponent at all, but like a friend.

Second, as we listen long and hard to what another person is saying, we gain real insight into that person's thinking. The longer we listen, the more we may become aware of those ideas or beliefs that are making trouble for the other person. Errors or false understandings become clear and we find a starting place for meaningful responses.

Third, if we are still more eager to listen than speak, we might respond to a person with questions instead of opinions of our own or criticisms. By asking important questions we can continue to demonstrate genuine concern and friendship while providing a means for the person to realize errors. Coming to new conclusions after thinking through things in our own minds is much more impressive than having someone shout an opinion at us (even if that person is right). God opened our ears by the Gospel so that we might do the same for others. Just as God often asked questions to bring people to their senses (e.g., Adam in Genesis 3:9; Job in Job 38–39; Pharisees in Matthew 22:41–46), so we follow His example in love.

The Power of Words

James offers strong counsel about speaking in 3:2–12 and 4:11–12. In these sections James condemns our tongue as a "world of evil," a "restless evil, full of deadly poison." James compares the tongue to a rudder of a ship or a flame that destroys a whole forest. How is it that so small a member in our body, speaking only words, is such a powerful force for harm?

The answer has to do with our bearing the image of God. For example, the Son of God is also called His Word (John 1:1, 14). God created and sustains all things by His Word. God's Word gives expression to who He is so that we might know Him.

We also are known by the words we speak. Jesus said, "Out of the overflow of the heart the mouth speaks" (Matthew 12:34). Since the fall of Adam, all human beings have wicked hearts, and that wickedness is expressed by the mouth. In particular, we speak in order to defend our lives and protect our power. So we express our own opinions vehemently while refusing to listen to others. We twist the truth of God's Word or ignore it in order to think and speak in ways that justify ourselves. We criticize and judge others because that gives us the impression that we are better than others. James condemns all of this, speaking in the clearest terms in order to do exactly what the Law should do: zipper our mouths so that we can listen to words of truth and grace (Romans 3:19–24).

How Could You Say Such a Thing?

Of all the regrets you have, how many have to do with things you wish you had never said? James expresses exasperation over the way we bless and curse with the same mouth. How can we do such things? The heart of the problem is your heart. Our heart is deceitful above all things and desperately wicked. Our mouth is the means by which that wicked heart expresses its pride and hatred. Surely every day of your life would be better if you could control that tongue of yours! But how?

Because God knows your heart, He determined to provide you with a new one through Baptism (Ezekiel 36:26). From a new heart springs forth rivers of living water (John 4:14). As long as the Word of the Lord dwells in you, you will have a heart like His. He has listened and will always listen carefully to your cries for help and speak for your deliverance. He announces the forgiveness of your sins and proclaims words of life to you. This is the source of your ability to listen to others, forsake wrath, and speak those words from the Lord that will genuinely help. ■

We've Got Plans!

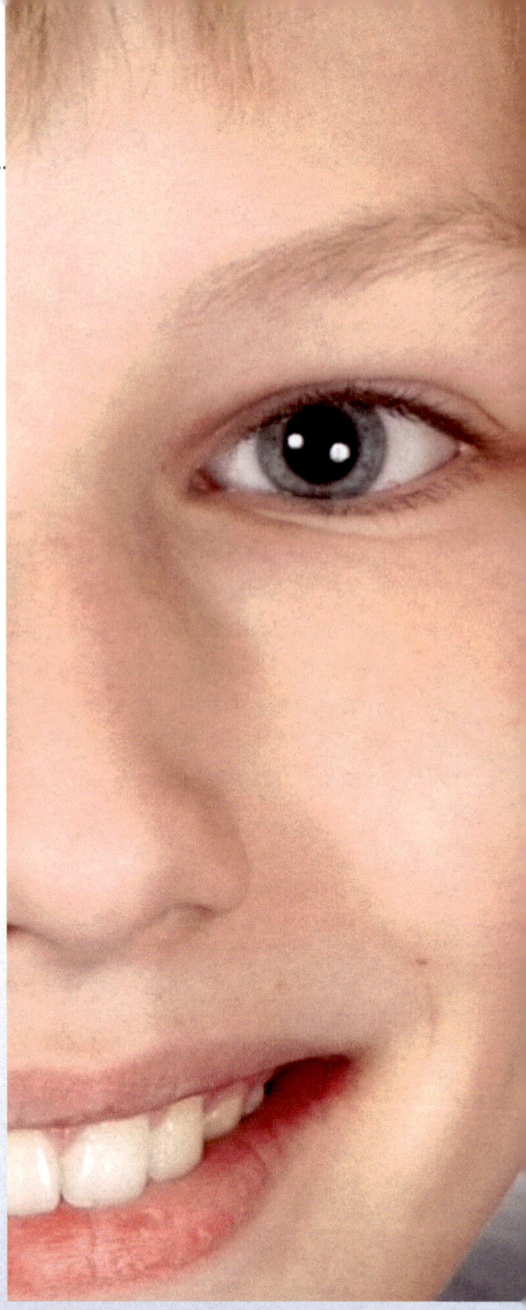

From the sunrise of life to its sunset, we make plans. James warns us about making plans for several reasons: (1) we don't know the future, (2) we often make plans that are contrary to our orientation or goals as Christians, and (3) we don't know the plans God has for us. Could James really be suggesting that you are better off not making plans at all?

Our Plans

James contends that people who make plans according to their human nature will indeed be sorry. He exposes problems with human planning. First, James does not seem impressed with people's plans to go here or there and make a profit. For James, such plans are too shortsighted.

Jesus expressed similar doubts about man-made plans. He told a parable of a man who had a tremendous harvest one year. Since the harvest was so large, the man decided to pull down his barns and build larger ones. He thought his life's work was done. Now he could live a relaxed, worry-free life of ease. However, that very night his life was required of him, so who would benefit from that harvest?

Jesus once asked, "What good will it be for a man if he gains the whole world, yet forfeits his soul?" (Matthew 16:26). In the same way James reminds us to think about the will of the Lord. The Lord's will has to do with things that are eternal and concern our whole life, not just short-term profits or goals.

Second, James recognizes that human plans are too often the product of boasting and arrogance. For example, King Herod once indulged his arrogance by allowing the citizens to call him a god (Acts 12:19–23). Herod was struck that very day with a miserable affliction that took his life. How could Herod consider himself a god if he was so vulnerable to human ailments?

Thinking too much of ourselves most often results in "entitlement" thinking. We may be disappointed, upset, or even angry with God when our plans don't work out, because

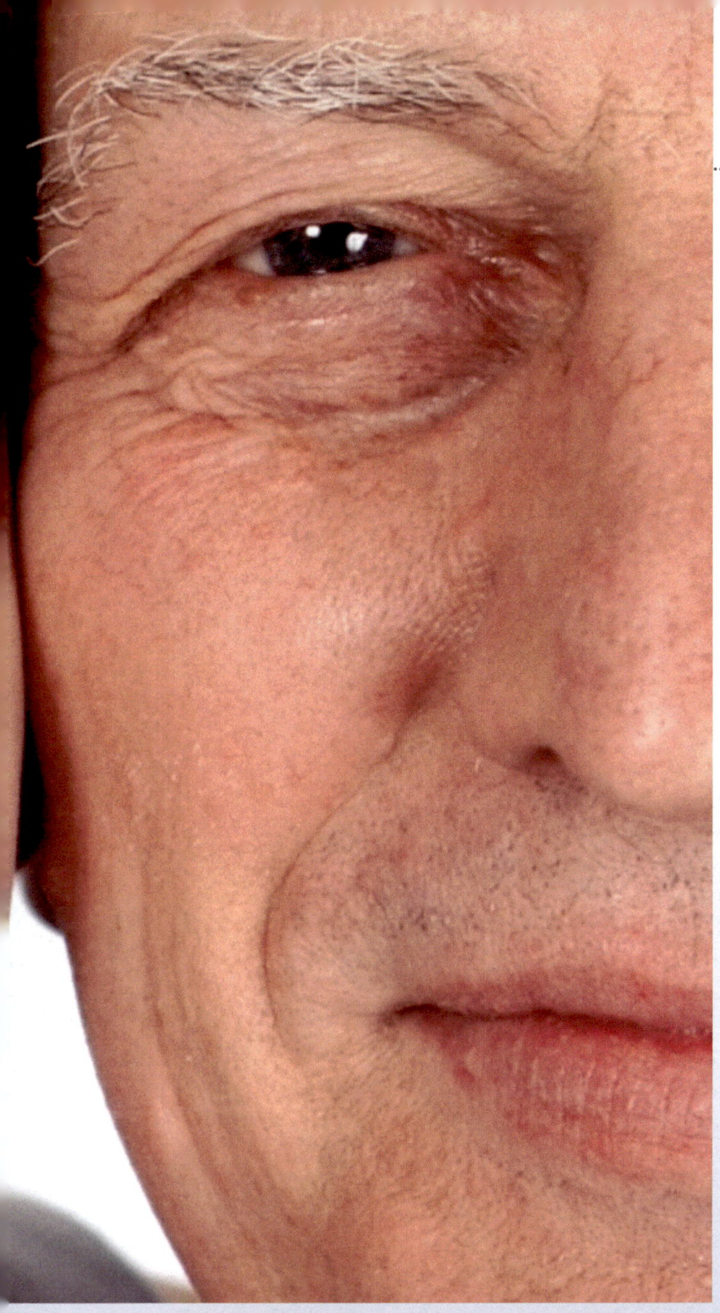

we feel like we are entitled to success. James hoped to spare his readers from spending their lives making plans in the wrong direction and suffering continual disappointments as a result.

God's Will Be Done

Does James then insist that we must never make plans? Not at all. James says that a Christian should always submit his or her thinking to the will of the Lord. Jesus gave us a reminder of this in the Lord's Prayer, "Thy will be done on earth as it is in heaven." Likewise, Paul wrote that the Lord provided the holy ministry to equip us to walk in the good works that God prepared for us from the foundation of the world (Ephesians 4:11–13).

But how can you know what God's will is when you make plans? Begin by keeping the big picture in mind. God desires all to be saved and come to the knowledge of the truth. Because of that will He has called us as witnesses for Christ, making His appeal to others through us. Therefore, every plan we make should find its purpose and value within that overall design.

Trust and Relax

Many students live with anxiety over what they should do after college. In particular, young Christian men and women often struggle with thoughts of becoming full-time church workers or serving God in some other way. This anxiety is greatly reduced if they remember two things. First, their whole life is a call to advance the Word and kingdom of God, no matter what they are doing in particular. Second, as students their call at this moment is to study and develop as fully as possible the talents that God has given them. What exactly that will mean for their future remains to be seen, and no amount of worry will make that known. What they *can* know is that God will not overlook a person whom He has gifted and prepared for service. If you are trained and ready to serve, the service will find you.

No doubt, James wrestled with such personal changes in plans himself. Before His oldest brother walked away from the family business, James probably anticipated life as an artisan and businessman. Watching Jesus walk away from the family business to live as a person with "no place to lay His head" (Matthew 8:20) must have disrupted James's own plans. Learning of Jesus' arrest and crucifixion may have crushed James's plans. But amid these changes God was planning something wonderful for James. He called him to preach the Gospel and even to lead the church in Jerusalem.

I Have Great Plans for You!

James issues a crushing blow to human arrogance by reminding us that our human life in this time is but a breath or mist (4:14). Solomon wrestled with this same truth in Ecclesiastes. After accomplishing plans of wealth, luxury, and fame, Solomon was disappointed. What would any of it mean? The end of his human life meant that he really did not posses any riches, could not control them after his death, and that they were really meaningless.

What have you spent your life accumulating or trying to accomplish? You can look ahead and see that any investment you have made in material things will eventually be lost. Solomon also wrote, "In his heart a man plans his course, but the LORD determines his steps" (Proverbs 16:9).

Knowing your life is but a breath is no cause for despair as long as you cling to the life that Christ has provided. In Christ you have a soul and spirit that live eternally. That life is about relationships and people. In Christ you have a lifelong purpose. Confidently make your plans in view of God's mercy. ■

Contend Steadfastly

Sometimes consequences are small. A person believes an advertisement for toothpaste that promises whiter teeth. If the advertisement is not true, the person will have lost a small amount of money. No big deal. But other times consequences are monumental. If a military operation is planned according to bad information, then many lives may be lost.

If Christians believe something that is not true, they, too, will suffer consequences. In view of this danger, Jude urges his readers to "contend for the faith" (v. 3). Jude's warning was necessary because the early Christians experienced so much opposition.

The Opposition

Jude lists the opposition Christians faced in his day: fallen angels (v. 6), the sexually immoral (v. 7), the devil (v. 9), the greedy (v. 11), the selfish (v. 12), and scoffers (v. 18). He shows that evil forces, both spiritual and material, continually surround and attack the people of God today. These forces are relentless in their opposition, never resting nor intending to give us rest. This is the reason Jude maintains that God's people must contend steadfastly!

However, contending does not mean we must be contentious people. To be contentious means to place ourselves in opposition to everyone. Being contentious means we cause division among others. Paul instructed Titus to warn contentious people two times before rejecting them (Titus 3:10). Contentious people do not serve God or others, but only their own peculiar ideas about what matters.

The "faith that was once for all entrusted to the saints" is how the saints know what matters and how they must take their stand. Knowing the one and only faith that is true and reveals a genuine redeemer is not something to let slip away. There is no substitute or replacement for this faith. So the saints contend steadfastly from conviction and from love. If we give up the faith, we are lost and are no longer any help to the rest of mankind.

Jude 6 speaks of the fate of fallen angels who once held to the truth but rebelled. They realized too late the eternal consequences of their rebellion. Since their fall these angels have continuously opposed the truth so that human beings would also fall from the truth and be lost. Therefore Jude holds up the faith "once for all" delivered to the saints.

Eternal Consequences

The Bible accurately conveys reality and is therefore truth. Jude speaks of it as "the faith," and not "a faith" or "faiths." The true faith was delivered once and for all because it never changes. At the center of that truth is the Son of God, who took upon Himself human nature in order to take our place under the Law. He fulfilled all that the Law required as He did right to all and as He suffered for all that everyone has done wrong. Through His Son God has provided for the salvation of the whole world. This faith is worth holding on to and the only means by which we hold on in this mad world.

Eternal Value

Every day people trade the timeless blessings of God for pleasures that are quick and easy. The pressure to believe that Jesus is just one option for faith among many is also ever present. Even worship today is characterized by the replacement of faithful liturgy and music with shallow content. In the rush to be relevant, sometimes the eternal value of the Gospel gets overlooked.

Jude is the shortest of all the general epistles in the New Testament, yet Jude's message is essential for you. Jude begins and ends with the essence of the faith once for all delivered: Jesus Christ, the only Lord, provides eternal life and is able to keep you from stumbling and present you faultless before His presence. This truth alone is able to inspire you with a conviction that endures. He has taken away your sins and has given you righteousness instead. Therefore, joyfully and eagerly contend steadfastly for this faith, not only because you are convinced that it alone provides truth and mercy, but because it also inspires in you a concern for others. The life He has given you is of immeasurable and enduring value. ■

The Value of Truth

A museum exhibit on pearls showed the difference between fake pearls, cultured pearls, and the most valuable kind, natural pearls. Fake pearls are easy to identify because they are made of glass, plastic, or other materials. Cultured pearls are more difficult to recognize because they are a combination of human activity and the natural process performed by shellfish. You may wonder why people create cultured pearls if they are not as good as natural pearls. The exhibit explained that people's love for pearls produced a demand for more and more. In other words, people's love for money drove them to create fakes.

James and Jude warn that people's love for money led to fake teachers in the early church. These brothers of Jesus highlight the importance of distinguishing between real teaching, which is the truth, and "cultured" teaching, which is false and the product of human invention.

Not Too Many Teachers

James warns that not too many people should seek to be teachers. James is not speaking of the teaching profession. James describes pastors and their work of speaking publicly on behalf of Christ (3:1–2). James provides a warning because those who would speak the Word in public on behalf of Christ will receive a stricter judgment.

The Word of God is the means by which His kingdom is extended to people. If God and His kingdom are present in His Word, it is no wonder that the devil continually makes this his point of attack. The devil's very first act was to contradict the Creator's Word. He undermined God's Word by contradicting God's instruction to Adam and Eve. Remember how the devil asked Eve, "Did God really say?" (Genesis 3:1). Nothing has changed. As James points out, the devil is still trying to contradict God's Word of life by false teachers and false teaching.

Jude also provides several severe warnings against false teachers. He reminds us that false teachers deny the Lord (Jude 4). This denial is consistent with the character of false teaching described in the opening. False teaching is driven by the desire for personal gain (Jude 11–12a). But no amount of false teaching can accumulate value or match the truth of God's Word.

The truth is that all people live in the poverty of rebellion against God. Life has no real value without Him. Many people try to obtain a substitute. Fallen human nature does this for two reasons. First, false teaching provides more of what people want in their effort to convince themselves that they have a life. Second, false teaching is popular and profitable.

Quality, not Quantity

The things we accumulate for ourselves cannot give life. Like fake pearls, material things have no eternal value. False teaching is of no value either. False teaching accepts some of God's truth but replaces it with human opinion in order to make it more acceptable to human thinking. Like cultured pearls, they look good but are not genuine.

If you have God's truth you know that there is no other. As you continue in God's truth you become able to recognize the falsehood of other teaching that would present itself as truth. The real beauty of God's truth is that as you share it with others, you are also keeping it for yourself. ■

Beware of False Teachers

You're only in trouble if you get caught

Example	Summary
Exodus from Egypt Jude 5a; Exodus 3–14	Jude begins with a positive example, how God rescued His people from Egypt.
Wilderness Rebellion Jude 5b; Exodus 15:22–17:7; 32:1–33:6; Numbers 11–12; 14;16; 20:1–13; Deuteronomy 1:26–46	Jude reminds his readers of how God did not fail to condemn and punish the sins of His chosen people.
Rebellion of the Angels Jude 6; Matthew 25:41; Luke 10:17–20; 2 Peter 2:4; Revelation 12	God punished Satan and the other fallen angels (demons) for rebelling against Him. Scripture does not give us many details about this rebellion. Jude 6 may describe Satan's temptation of Adam and Eve (Genesis 3) or an earlier event.
Sodom and Gomorrah Jude 7; Genesis 18:16–19:29	The wickedness of these cities brought their destruction.
Burial of Moses Jude 9; Deuteronomy 34	God did not allow Moses to enter the Promised Land because he rebelled. Jude records a detail about the spiritual battle surrounding Moses and rebukes the false teachers for their abusive talk.
Cain's Way Jude 11; Genesis 4:1–16	Cain murdered his brother and became a lasting example of those who profess care but harbor hatred (1 John 2:9–11; 3:11–15).
Balaam's Error Jude 11; 2 Peter 2:15; Numbers 22–24	Balaam sought financial gain through false teaching. Jude recognizes the same motive in the hearts of the false teachers in his day (Jude 17–19).
Korah's Rebellion Jude 11; Numbers 16:1–3, 31–35	Korah stirred up other Israelites against Moses and Aaron because they were experiencing hard times. Note Jude's description of the false teachers in his day (Jude 16).
Enoch's Prophecy Jude 14–15; Genesis 5:18–24	Note the fourfold repetition of "ungodly." Enoch's prophecy emphasizes God's call to holiness in contrast to the "ungodly" false teachers.

The saying "You're only in trouble if you get caught" is popular and may be heard in many different contexts. Teenagers often have this idea firmly in their minds as they "try" something forbidden. News reports may leave us with the definite impression that some political figures or business tycoons live according to this principle. The idea of doing wrong without fear of punishment has always been popular among wrongdoers and despised by advocates of real justice. Jude responds to both groups with clear expressions of God's judgment against all wrongdoing. Though false teachers and lying prophets wrap themselves in the mantle of faithfulness and innocence, no one escapes the justice of God.

In so short a letter, with only 25 verses, Jude cites nine different examples of God's judgment from the Old Testament! Read the chart to learn how this teaching applies to your life.

Application
Our lives as Christians begin with God's decisive action, rescuing us through His Son, Jesus Christ. He then calls us to lead honorable lives as we await the fullness of His mercy (Jude 21).
Just because we are God's people doesn't mean we are immune from His judgment or discipline. In fact, because we are God's people, we can count on receiving His discipline! The Lord desires that we encourage and sustain one another until He comes again (Jude 22–23).
If God punishes angels for abandoning their callings, will He spare others when they rebel against Him? (Consider God's punishment for the ruler of Babylon in Isaiah 14:3–21, which prefigures the punishment of the "beast" or "Satan" on the Last Day.)
God's punishment of these cities for sexual immorality serves as a warning for us today. The Lord calls us to faithfulness, modesty, and mercy (Jude 22–23).
A spiritual battle surrounds you today. Yet the Lord can keep you faithful through Christ (Jude 1). God grant you the faith of Moses and the modest words of Michael.
God grant you love for your brothers and sisters in the Gospel. He will keep you from falling (Jude 24).
Christian, mind how you exercise your life's calling and do not support false teachers with your dollars. (Think especially of the outrageous profits people make from false predictions about the end of the world.)
An important aspect of Moses' leadership was humility (Numbers 16:4). Look for this attribute in the leadership at your congregation. Pray for your leaders and support them (Hebrews 13:17).
The One who calls you to holiness will also present you before the heavenly Father "without fault" (Jude 24). By the cross, He has removed all your guilt.

The judgment of God against ungodliness is inescapable, but that is not His only judgment. God executed judgment against His own Son in our stead. The fact that God's judgment fell upon Christ as our substitute means that He can provide yet another judgment for those who are in Christ. God's Word connects us with Christ and judges us "not guilty." His Word generates a whole new being within us. This new being has a heart and mind like Christ.

Three times in his short letter Jude anticipates the glorious return of his brother Jesus (vv. 14, 21, 24). Because of the new heart and life you have received, you, too, can joyfully anticipate Jesus' return. United with Christ in your Baptism you have already passed through judgment and are living an eternal life. The ungodliness of your human nature is forgiven. The godliness that your Creator intended for you is present in your life by the work of the Holy Spirit through the Word. By the grace of God everyone will get what they have coming. Those who are in Christ will receive the fulfillment of all the promises of God for life in this world and forever after. ■

Study Guide

LifeLight

LifeLight Expands

Available NOW!

The Bible: An Overview
Genesis, Pt. 1
Genesis, Pt. 2
Exodus, Pt. 1
Exodus, Pt. 2
Wilderness Wanderings
Joshua
Judges
Ruth/Esther
1 & 2 Samuel
Life of David
1 & 2 Kings
1 & 2 Chronicles
Ezra/Nehemiah
Job
Selected Psalms
Proverbs
Ecclesiastes/ Song of Solomon
Isaiah, Pt. 1
Isaiah, Pt. 2
Jeremiah/Lamentations
Ezekiel
Daniel
Hosea/Joel/Amos
Obadiah/Jonah/Micah
Minor Prophets
Nahum/Habakkuk/ Zephaniah
Haggai/Zechariah/ Malachi
Matthew, Pt. 1
Matthew, Pt. 2
Mark
Luke, Pt. 1
Luke, Pt. 2
John, Pt. 1
John, Pt. 2
Acts, Pt. 1
Acts, Pt. 2
Romans, Pt. 1
Romans, Pt. 2
1 Corinthians
2 Corinthians
Galatians/Philippians/ Colossians
Ephesians/ 1 & 2 Thessalonians
Timothy/Titus/Philemon
Hebrews
James/Jude
1 & 2 Peter
1, 2, 3 John
Revelation

LifeLight Foundations

Baptism
Bible Feasts
Creation, New Creation
The Christian's Mission
End Times
Heaven & Hell
Law & Gospel
Ministry
Miracles
Parables
Prayer
Prophecy
Time between the Testaments
Triune God
Worship

Dealing with Trials and Temptations

Distribute before session 1 for use in session 1.
Use Enrichment Magazine pages 2–7.

James 1:1–18; Matthew 13:53–58; 12:46–49; 14:22–34

Resources for Worship

Use these resources for your daily study at home and at the week's assembly.

Hymn

Entrust your days and burdens
To God's most loving hand;
He cares for you while ruling
The sky, the sea, the land.
He that in clouds and tempest
Finds breakthrough for the sun
Will find right pathways for you
Till trav'ling days are done.

Leave all to God's direction;
His wisdom rules for you
In ways to rouse your wonder
At all His love can do.
When His plans are maturing,
Then wonder-working pow'rs
Will banish from your spirit
What gave you troubled hours.

Paul Gerhardt; tr. F. Samuel Janzow

Prayer

Lord, You know how confused we become when the hard things of life come our way and how quickly we give in when sin beckons. Help us to see these things for what they really are and to count on You to keep us strong. In Your own great name we pray. Amen.

Digging Deep
My Personal Study for Week 1

Day 1 • Read James 1:1; Matthew 13:53–58; 12:46–49

1. The author of the epistle of James identifies himself simply as "James, a servant of God and of the Lord Jesus Christ" (v. 1). Several important followers of Jesus bore that name—the son of Zebedee (Matthew 4:21); James the Less, son of Alphaeus (Matthew 10:3); and the one referred to in the passages listed above, who appears to be the author of this letter.

a. What does Matthew 13:53–58 tell us about his *human* relationship to Jesus?

b. What does James 1:1 tell us about his *spiritual* relationship to Jesus?

2. a. What was James's initial reaction to Jesus' ministry (John 7:5)?

b. How did Jesus feel about this (Matthew 12:46–49)?

c. Why do you suppose James did not identify himself as a human relative of Jesus in this letter?

3. According to 1 Corinthians 15:3–8 what happened to change James's attitude toward Jesus?

4. a. What position did James hold in the Jerusalem congregation (Acts 15:6–21)?

b. Why might this give his letter authority among the Christians outside of Jerusalem?

Day 2 • Read James 1:2–8, 12

5. In James 1:2 the author refers to various kinds of trials that test the faith of his readers. If his readers are the same people mentioned in Acts 8:1–3 and 11:19 (and they probably are), what were the trials and troubles that they were experiencing? See Acts 22:4 and 19 and 26:10 for some specifics.

6. a. What is perseverance (v. 3)?

b. How does the testing of trouble and hardship produce it (v. 3)?

7. a. What or who is the "wisdom" referred to in verses 5–8?

b. How may it help us to deal with our trials?

1 Corinthians 1:21–25

Colossians 2:2–3

Hebrews 2:10–17

8. We are told to rejoice in our trials and persecutions because they produce perseverance (vv. 3–4) and can lead to the crown of life (v. 12). Elsewhere in Scripture we are given other reasons for such rejoicing. What are they?

Acts 5:41

Listening and Responding

Distribute before session 2 for use in session 2.
Use Enrichment Magazine pages 14–18.

James 1:19–2:13; John 15:5–17; Colossians 3:1–16; Romans 6:1–14; Luke 6:20–26; Matthew 25:31–46

Resources for Worship

Use the resources for daily study at home and at the week's assembly.

Hymn

Speak, O Lord, Your servant listens,
Let Your Word to me come near;
Newborn life and Spirit give me,
Let each promise still my fear.
Death's dread pow'r, its inward strife,
Wars against Your Word of life;
Fill me, Lord, with love's strong fervor
That I cling to You forever!

Oh, what blessing to be near You
And to listen to Your voice;
Let me ever love and hear You,
Let Your Word be now my choice!
Many hardened sinners, Lord,
Flee in terror at Your Word,
But to me, who know my burden,
Show me now Your Word of pardon!

Precious Jesus, I entreat You,
Let Your words in me take root;
Let this gift of heav'n enrich me
So that I bring gen'rous fruit:
Never take them from my heart
Till I see You as You are,
When in heav'nly bliss and glory
I will meet You and adore You!

Anna Sophia of Hesse-Darmstadt; tr. George T. Rygh

Prayer

Heavenly Father, how grateful we are for Your Word, for revealing Your heart to us in that Word, for reaching out to us with love and hope and guidance. Forgive us for being such poor listeners. Give us open ears and minds as we study Your Word, and help us always to respond with believing hearts and obedient lives. We dare to ask this in the name and for the sake of Your Son and our Savior, Jesus. Amen.

Digging Deep
My Personal Study for Week 2

Day 1 • Read James 1:19–21; John 15:5–17

1. a. What does James mean when he urges us to "be quick to listen, slow to speak" in verse 19? See verse 26.

b. What is the opposite of this?

c. Why is it so important for us to listen? See John 15:5–17.

2. a. What are we supposed to listen to?

b. What effect will it have upon us? See verses 18, 21, 25; 2:12; and John 8:31.

c.What kind of freedom is referred to in these passages?

d. From what and for what are we set free?

3. Where is that Word located? See verse 21; John 5:39.

4. What, or who, is the specific content of that Word? See 1:18; John 1:14; Romans 10:17.

Day 2 • Read James 1:19–22; Colossians 3:1–16; Romans 6:1–14

5. God's Word is calculated to produce a response in us. If we listen to it and take it to heart, we will be able to make some important changes. God the Holy Spirit makes this possible. How do angry, immoral, and arrogant attitudes (vv. 20–22) interfere with the response that God intends and enables?

6. When we let evil attitudes have their way, who actually is in control of us? See Romans 6:12 and Colossians 3:5.

7. How will these attitudes and the actions that flow from them affect our ability to listen to God?

8. According to Romans 6:1–14 and Colossians 3:1–16 what resources do we have for dealing with evil attitudes and inclinations?

Day 3 • Read James 1:23–27; 2:10–11

9. As we listen to God's Word and accept it by faith, it is planted in our hearts (v. 21). It is there for us, not only when we are in the process of listening or reading, but also when we do other things. How can we get access to and draw benefit from that implanted Word?

10. In order to help us break free from the controlling power of sin, God's Word first exposes our sins and makes us aware of them. This part of God's Word is called "the Law."

a. How does the reference to the mirror illustrate this (vv. 23–24)?

Faith in Action

Distribute before session 3 for use in session 3.
Use Enrichment Magazine pages 10–12.

James 2:14–26; Ephesians 2:4–10; 1 John 3:16–18; Genesis 22:1–19; Hebrews 11:17–19, 31; Joshua 2:1–21

Resources for Worship

Use these resources for daily worship at home and for the week's assembly.

Hymn

Renew Me, O eternal Light,
And let my heart and soul be bright,
Illumined with the light of grace
That issues from Your holy face.

Remove the pow'r of sin from me
And cleanse all my impurity
That I may have the strength and will
Temptations of the flesh to still.

Create in me a new heart, Lord,
That gladly I obey Your Word.
Let what You will be my desire,
And with new life my soul inspire.

Grant that I only You may love
And seek those things which are above
Till I behold You face to face,
O Light eternal, through Your grace.

Johann F. Ruopp, tr. August Crull, alt.

Prayer

Awaken and energize our faith, O Lord, so that all we say and do may reflect Your presence and influence. Deliver us from the kind of complacency that is satisfied only to "talk the talk." Forgive us by Your own sacrifice and transform us by Your Spirit so that our faith in You may be translated into loving action toward those around us. In Your own powerful name we pray. Amen.

Digging Deep
My Personal Study for Week 3

Day 1 • Read James 2:14–26; Ephesians 2:4–10

1. Many readers, even scholars, are confused and troubled by this section because James appears to be contradicting Paul, or vice versa. Carefully compare the verses from Ephesians with the verses from James. Against which *false* point of view is James speaking?

2. Against which *false* point of view is Paul speaking?

3. Does Paul say that the performance of good works is important or necessary for a believer?

4. Does James say that good works save?

Day 2 • Read James 2:14–17; 1 John 3:16–18

5. How does James describe authentic, saving faith?

6. How does he describe phony, unauthentic faith?

7. What, according to 1 John 3:16–18, is the motivation for faith in action?

8. In what ways do we sometimes show that we are satisfied with inactive faith? Give some specific examples.

Day 3 • Read James 2:18–19

9. Think carefully about verse 18. Explain more fully the false point of view expressed here.

10. What is wrong with that point of view? Explain your answer as much as you can.

11. What is the proper relationship between faith and deeds? See also Hebrews 11:6 and 2 Corinthians 3:18.

Taming the Tongue

Distribute before session 4 for use in session 4.
Use Enrichment Magazine pages 21–23.

James 3:1–12; Ephesians 4:29–32; 5:4–6, 19–20; Mark 6:14–29

Resources for Worship

Use these resources for daily worship at home and at the week's assembly.

Hymn

Oh, bless the Lord, my soul!
Let all in me combine
To aid my tongue to bless His name
Whose favor is divine.

The Lord forgives my sins,
And He relieves my pain;
The Lord has healed my sicknesses
And made me whole again.

He crowns my life with love,
He ransoms from the grave;
He that redeemed my soul from hell
Has sov'reign pow'r to save.

His works and laws and ways
He made by Moses known
But showed the world His loving heart
In Christ, His only Son.

Isaac Watts, alt.

Prayer

We thank You, Heavenly Father, for the magnificent gift of speech by which we can share our thoughts and feelings with others and even praise You and share You with others. Help us always to use our tongues for these good purposes and to resist the temptation to use them in destructive ways. Forgive us for letting our tongues get out of control and make them instead instruments of Your Spirit. In Jesus' name we pray. Amen.

Digging Deep
My Personal Study for Week 4

Day 1 • Read Ephesians 4:29–32; 5:4–6, 19–20

1. What are the important *purposes* for which God has given us the gift of speech? Look through all verses listed above.

2. What *qualities* or *characteristics* should our speech exhibit? Check the Ephesians verses for this too.

3. What *sinful* kinds of speech should we avoid?

4. What *motivation* does Paul use? See especially Ephesians 4:32; 5:2; 5:18.

Day 2 • Read James 3:1–2

5. What are some valid reasons for wanting to be a teacher of God's Word?

6. What are some ways in which a teacher may stumble?

7. Why is a teacher of God's Word judged more strictly than other Christians?

8. What do you think are the rewards of being a teacher?

9. *For personal reflection. Sharing optional.* Think about some of the people who by deeds and words were most influential in teaching and nurturing you in your Christian faith and life. What was it that you most appreciated in them? Breathe a prayer of thanks to God for each of them.

Day 3 • Read James 3:3–6; Mark 6:14–29

10. In this section James is pointing out that what we say, for better or for worse, very often determines what we will do. Explain how the Mark passage bears this out.

Dealing with Conflict

Distribute before session 5 for use in session 5.
Use Enrichment Magazine pages 19–20, 28–29.

James 3:13–4:12

Resources for Worship

Use these resources for your daily study and at the week's assembly.

Hymn

Love divine, all love excelling,
Joy of heav'n, to earth come down!
Fix in us Thy humble dwelling,
All Thy faithful mercies crown.

Jesus, Thou art all compassion,
Pure, unbounded love thou art;
Visit us with Thy salvation,
Enter ev'ry trembling heart.

Breathe, oh, breathe Thy loving Spirit
Into ev'ry troubled breast;
Let us all in Thee inherit;
Let us find Thy promised rest.
Take away the love of sinning;
Alpha and Omega be;
End of faith, as its beginning,
Set our hearts at liberty.

Charles Wesley

Prayer

How it must grieve You, Lord Jesus, when we, Your followers, quarrel and fight. You love us all and make us one in You, and yet, in our sinfulness we sometimes violate this unity and disturb that fellowship. In Your mercy forgive these wrongs and make us right in Your sight. Heal the wounds we inflict on our relationships with one another. By the power of Your love, help us to love and serve one another in humility as You love and serve us. Amen.

Digging Deep
My Personal Study for Week 5

Day 1 • Read James 3:13–18

1. Verse 13 calls us to examine our own life. Does our life show deeds done in humility? How do we *get* "the humility that comes from wisdom"? See James 1:5 and Matthew 11:28–30.

2. Verse 14 identifies two enemies of true wisdom and humility that begin in the heart, our old sinful nature. How do we resist and overcome such temptation? See Romans 13:14.

3. *For personal reflection. Sharing optional.* Think about your interactions with people during the past few days or week—not only with those who are near and dear, but also with those who rub you the wrong way. Confess to God any instances when you were less than humble and loving; when "envy and selfish ambition" took over. Then, in the confidence that these sins have been covered in the righteousness of Christ, thank your heavenly Father for His forgiveness and ask Him to enable you to grow in godly wisdom and behavior.

4. Re-read verses 15–18. Then read 1 Corinthians 2:6–16 for a commentary on the wisdom that comes "from heaven," from God the Holy Spirit, and the wisdom that comes from the devil and his world. What verses are especially meaningful to you?

5. a. How does peacemaking lead to "righteousness"—the conduct that is pleasing to God (v. 18)? Refer back to James 1:19–20.

b. What does our Lord promise to peacemakers? See Matthew 5:9.

Day 2 • Read James 4:1–3

6. What does verse 1 say is the source of the fights and quarrels among James' Christian readers?

7. a. According to Romans 7:21–25, what "part" of us Christians delights in God's Law?

b. What part fights against our delight in God's Law? (See also Titus 3:3.)

c. Who rescues us from this "body of death" (Romans 7:24)?

8. Verse 2 points out the terrible things that frustrated desire can lead to. How do Matthew 5:21–22 and 1 John 3:15 underscore the seriousness of these desires?

Manipulated by Money

Distribute before session 6 for use in session 6.
Use Enrichment Magazine pages 12–13, 24–26.

James 4:13–5:6; Luke 12:16–21; Malachi 3:5

Resources for Worship

Use the resources for daily worship at home and at the week's assembly.

Hymn

Come, you thankful people, come;
Raise the song of harvest home.
All is safely gathered in
Ere the winter storms begin.
God, our maker, does provide
For our wants to be supplied.
Come to God's own temple, come,
Raise the song of harvest home.

For the Lord our God shall come
And shall take His harvest home,
From His field shall in that day
All offenses purge away,
Give His angels charge at last
In the fire the tares to cast
But the fruitful ears to store
In His garner evermore.

Even so, Lord, quickly come
To Your final harvest home.
Gather all Your people in,
Free from sorrow, free from sin,
There, forever purified,
In Your garner to abide.
Come, with all Your angels, come,
Raise the glorious harvest home.

Henry Alford

Prayer

Your generosity, O Lord, is overwhelming. You lovingly pour into our lives the money and other material things that we need. Help us always to recognize You and Your love in these things, and move us to use them faithfully. Forgive us for so often making an idol of money, that which we don't have as well as that which we do have. Direct us by your Spirit to use our wealth in ways that honor You and help others, so that money is always our servant and not our master. In Jesus' name we pray. Amen.

Digging Deep
My Personal Study for Week 6

Day 1 • Read James 4:13–14; Luke 12:16–21

1. What false assumptions about the future and money are reflected in these passages?

2. How do these assumptions lead to boasting?

3. What kind of business did the people have to whom James is speaking in these verses?

4. How does Jesus respond to their false assumption?

5. What do you suppose is meant by being "rich toward God"? See Luke 12:31–34.

Day 2 • Read James 4:15

6. What is the Lord's connection to the future and money?

7. How should we respond to this?

8. Is James condemning wealth and those who plan and work to obtain it? Consider, again, James 1:10–11. See also Matthew 19:23–26.

9. What is James condemning?

Day 3 • Read James 4:16–17

10. What is the good that we should be doing with our money? Reconsider the circumstances of James's readers, as discussed in the last session.

11. How were the readers whom James admonishes being manipulated by money?

Patience

Distribute before session 7 for use in session 7.
Use Enrichment Magazine pages 8–9.

James 5:7–20; 2 Peter 3:8–9; Ephesians 4:2–6; Psalms 22 and 38; Job 1:21–22; Hebrews 2:17–18; Romans 8:18, 28; Matthew 5:34–37

Resources for worship

Use these resources for daily worship at home and for the week's assembly.

Hymn

God moves in a mysterious way
His wonders to perform;
He plants His footsteps in the sea
And rides upon the storm.

Judge not the Lord by feeble sense,
But trust Him for His grace;
Behind a frowning providence
Faith sees a smiling face.

Blind unbelief is sure to err
And scan His work in vain;
God is His own interpreter,
And He will make it plain.

You fearful saints, fresh courage take;
The clouds you so much dread
Are big with mercy and will break
In blessing on your head.

William Cowper, alt.

Prayer

Heavenly Father, waiting is hard for us. It disturbs us when nothing seems to happen to relieve our suffering, solve our problems, or straighten out the people who cause us grief. You are so patient with us, and we take comfort in that. Create in us the readiness to wait for You to act in Your own time and way to answer our prayers and respond to our needs. We know that You are listening because Your Son invited us to pray and assured us that You will open Your heart to us. Amen.

Digging Deep
My Personal Study for Week 7

Day 1 • Read James 5:7–9; 2 Peter 3:8–9

1. What were some aspects of James's readers' situation that required special patience? Scan the entire letter and your notes made for the previous sessions. Jot down some highlights here.

2. How does the Lord's promise to return encourage patience?

3. How does the farmer's waiting for rain compare with the Christian's waiting for the Lord's return?

4. How does Peter explain the apparent delay in Christ's return? See 2 Peter 3:8–9.

Day 2 • Read James 5:9a, 13–20; Ephesians 4:2–6

5. Why were some of James's readers apparently grumbling about one another? Refer again to the references about their situation mentioned above.

6. Instead of grumbling about one another, James urges us to respond in constructive ways. What are these, according to 5:13–20?

7. What, according to Paul in Ephesians 4:2, are some important aspects of the patience we are to have with one another?

8. What does Paul give us as the basis for patience with one another in Ephesians 4:3–6?

Day 3 • Read James 5:10–11; Psalm 22; Psalm 38; Job 1:21–22; Hebrews 2:17–18; Romans 8:18, 28

9. What kinds of suffering were James's readers experiencing? Refer again to their situation as we have discussed it in previous sessions.

10. From Psalm 22 and/or Psalm 38, as well as from your own experience and that of others, what are aspects of suffering that make it so challenging?

11. James refers here to patience and perseverance. They are closely related. Perseverance means to remain faithful to God, confident and hopeful, while putting up with suffering, in the way that the martyrs did. How did Job exhibit this kind of patience (1:21–22)?

Contending for the Truth

Distribute before session 8 for use in session 8.
Use Enrichment Magazine pages 26–27.

Jude 1–16; 2 Peter 2

Resources for Worship

Use these resources for your daily worship and at the week's assembly.

Hymn

Send, O Lord, Your Holy Spirit
On Your servant now, we pray;
Let him prove a faithful shepherd
That no lamb is led astray.
Your pure teaching to proclaim,
To extol Your holy name,
And to feed Your lambs, dear Savior,
Make his aim and sole endeavor.

You, O Lord, Yourself have called him
For Your precious lambs to care;
But to prosper in his calling,
He the Spirit's gifts must share.
Give him wisdom from above,
Fill his heart with holy love;
In his weakness, Lord, be near him,
In his prayers, Good Shepherd, hear him.

Help, Lord Jesus, help him nourish
All our children with Your Word
That in fervent love they serve You
Till in heav'n their song is heard,
Boundless blessings, Lord, bestow
On his faithful toil below
Till by grace to him be given
His reward, the crown of heaven.

Author unknown; tr. Frederick W. Herzberger, alt.

Prayer

Heavenly Father, we are most grateful for the many faithful pastors and teachers of Your Word with which You have blessed Your church. We pray that Your Word may make an indelible impression on us so that we are never misled from it. Help us to discern and reject the false teachings and influences that we are exposed to and to embrace Your truth as our salvation and as our guide to life. In Jesus' name we pray. Amen.

Digging Deep
My Personal Study for Week 8

Day 1 • Read Jude 1–4; 2 Peter 2

1. a. How does a comparison between Jude 1 and James 1:1 help you to identify the author?

b. What further information do you find in Matthew 13:55–56 and John 7:5?

2. We don't know how Jude became a believer, but reflect on 1 Corinthians 15:7 and John 1:40–42 for a possibility and on Acts 1:14 for the spiritual status of other family members.

3. Read 2 Peter 2 and note the similarities with Jude 3–16.

4. Compare Jude 18 and 2 Peter 3:3. What does this tell us about the relationship of Jude to 2 Peter?

Day 2 • Read Jude 3–4

5. According to these verses what is the difference between what Jude wanted to write and what he did write?

6. a. How did the false teachers get into the church and become influential?

b. In what way did they deny Jesus? See Titus 1:16.

7. What was the heart of their false teaching?

8. What is meant by "the faith" (v. 3)? See these verses:

Philippians 1:27

1 Timothy 4:6

Day 3 • Read Jude 5–7

9. What were the offenses of the three groups mentioned in verses 5–7 and the divine judgments that fell upon each?

10. Summarize the sin and punishment of Sodom and Gomorrah (Genesis 19:1–29).

11. Terrible and frightening are the images we receive in verses 5–7, all pointing to those who "suffer the punishment of eternal fire."

a. We've all been frightened by the dark. What is frightening about the thought of the "blackest darkness" (Jude 6, 13; Matthew 8:12)?

Dealing with Scoffers

Distribute before session 9 for use in session 9.
Use Enrichment Magazine pages 30–32.

Jude 17–25; 2 Peter 3:3–4

Resources for worship

Use these resources for your daily study at home and at the week's assembly.

Hymn

Lo, on those who dwelt in darkness,
Dark as night and deep as death,
Broke the light of Thy salvation,
Breathed Thine own life-giving breath.
Alleluia, alleluia!
Praise to Thee who light dost send!
Alleluia, alleluia!
Alleluia without end!

Give us lips to sing Thy glory,
Tongues Thy mercy to proclaim,
Throats that shout the hope that fills us,
Mouths to speak Thy holy name.
Alleluia, alleluia!
May the light which Thou dost send!
Fill our songs with alleluias,
Alleluias without end!

God the Father, light-creator,
To Thee laud and honor be.
To Thee, Light of Light begotten,
Praise be sung eternally.
Holy Spirit, light-revealer,
Glory, glory, be to Thee.
Mortals, angels, now and ever
Praise the holy Trinity!

Martin H. Franzmann

Prayer

Heavenly Father, give us the kind of loyalty and faithfulness to the truth of Your Word that will make us ready to stand up for it whenever and wherever it is threatened or attacked. By Your Holy Spirit help us to understand and grasp Your truth so firmly that no one will ever be able to lead us astray. Forgive us the indifference and negligence that make us ready to compromise Your truth or to tolerate its corruption. Give us the patience and the love that we need to effectively reach out to those who are misguided or wavering. In Jesus' name we pray. Amen

Digging Deep
My Personal Study for Week 9

Day 1 • Read Jude 17–19; 2 Peter 3:2–4

1. According to verse 17, why should Jude's readers not have been surprised by the troublemakers who appeared in their midst?

2. What do the following texts add to the picture?

2 Peter 3:2–4

Acts 20:29

1 Timothy 4:1–5

3. What is the source of their scoffing?

4. How and why do they have such a detrimental effect on the church?

Day 2 • Read Jude 18; 2 Peter 3:3–4

5. "To scoff" is "to make fun of." What, according to 2 Peter 3:3–4 were they making fun of?

6. How do scoffers want to make Christians feel?

7. What other reasons may people have for scoffing?

8. *For personal reflection. Sharing optional.* Think about a time when you experienced someone scoffing at your Christian faith. How did you feel—stupid, frightened, sorry for the scoffer, or . . . ? What did you say or do? How did (or could) the Holy Spirit help you to respond?

Day 3 • Read Jude 20–21

9. How can reinforced faith support us in the struggle against scoffers and other enemies of the truth?

10. How can we build ourselves up in our most holy faith and keep ourselves in God's love? See these verses:

Romans 8:35–39

Colossians 3:15–16

11. How can Spirit-guided prayer support us?

12. How can God's love in Christ support us?

13. When will the struggle be over? See Matthew 25:31–34, 46.

Day 4 • Read Jude 22–23

14. Why was it necessary for Jude to urge his readers to be merciful toward those who were taken in by the scoffers?

15. How should they regard them? See Galatians 6:1–2.

16. What is the "fire" from which "others" should be snatched? See Amos 4:11.

17. How should we feel about scoffers and their influence? (Note: A better translation of "mercy" [v. 23] is "pity.")

Day 5 • Read Jude 24–25

18. As we struggle against scoffers and other enemies of the truth, and sometimes are taken in by them, to what can we look forward?

19. Because God is able to keep us from falling, does this mean that we will never fall? Use these verses to explain your answer:

Romans 7:21–25

Romans 6:4

20. What will make it possible for us to be faultless in God's presence when Christ returns in glory? See Colossians 1:21–22.

21. *For personal meditation.* Slowly reread this closing doxology (vv. 24–25), thinking of the meaning of the words as *your own* in praise and adoration of our wonderful God.

b. We've all experienced the terror of sudden separation from a loved one—perhaps from a parent who has lost us in a store. What's so frightening about the thought of being separated—forever—from God? See Matthew 25:41.

c. Probably the most painful injury we've all experienced is that of a burn. What's so frightening about the thought of being in "eternal fire" (Jude 7; Matthew 25:41)?

d. *For personal reflection. Sharing optional.* What are some of the joys *you* especially look forward to as you meditate on such texts as John 3:16; Matthew 25:45–46; John 10:27–29?

Day 4 • Read Jude 8–10

12. In what way did the false teachers "pollute their own bodies"? See Jude 4, 7, and 1 Corinthians 6:18–19.

13. From Deuteronomy 34:5–6 we know that the Lord buried Moses. Jude 9 tells us that God used the archangel Michael as His servant to bury the prophet. Why might the devil have challenged Michael? One possible speculation is that God may have raised Moses from the dead—and that's why the devil was contending for the *decay* of that body. How do 2 Kings 2:11 and Matthew 17:1–4 support that possibility?

14. What underlies the arrogant denial of God's truth of these enemies of the Gospel, as outlined in these verses?

a. 2 Peter 2:12

b. 1 Corinthians 2:14

Day 5 • Read Jude 11–16

15. Verse 11 gives three Old Testament examples of the kind of people whose example we need to avoid. Use these verses to give a short explanation of each:

a. "the way of Cain"—Genesis 4:5–8; Hebrews 11:4; 1 John 3:12

b. "Balaam's error"—2 Peter 2:15–16

c. "Korah's rebellion"—Numbers 16:1–3, 31–35

16. In six graphic metaphors, verses 12–13 depict the sin and the ultimate punishment of the false teachers.

a. List the six metaphors.

b. Which of these seems most graphic and powerful to you?

17. In verse 14, Jude refers to a nonbiblical ancient writing that was well-known and respected by early Christians.

a. What reasons might Jude have had for quoting a nonbiblical source? See also these verses:

b. Acts 17:28

c. Titus 1:12

12. In Job 6–7 we see that he also complained to God, as have many believers, and God puts up with that. However, God also offers strength, hope, and comfort to us when we suffer. What do the following passages say about this?

Hebrews 2:17–18

Romans 8:18, 28?

13. *For personal reflection. Sharing optional.* Reflect on one or more times in your life when you experienced real suffering—a time when your faith and trust in God were challenged. Looking back on that experience now, what strength and comfort from Scripture helped you to survive and even grow spiritually from the experience?

Day 4 • Read James 5:12; Matthew 5:34–37

14. Swearing here means taking oaths in God's name, but James's words also apply to other ways of taking God's name in vain. What are some reasons why we might use God's name wrongly in an oath or in other statements?

15. How is an oath by heaven or earth connected with God's name?

16. The prohibition given here is related to the use of God's name in trivial matters. Under what circumstances is it good and right to use God's name? See these verses:

Psalm 34:3

Acts 2:21

Matthew 28:19

Can you think of others?

17. How may the misuse of God's name be evidence of impatience? (This will require some special thought.)

Day 5 • Read James 5:13–18

18. In 1:19 James tells us to be "quick to listen." In these verses he is telling us to be quick to pray. They discuss an area that requires holy *impatience*. In what situations should we be quick to pray?

19. What was the significance of the oil that was to be applied when praying for the sick? See Luke 10:34 and Mark 6:13.

20. What is the power of prayer as described in these verses? See also 1 Kings 17:1 and 18:1.

21. What does Jesus' prayer in Gethsemane (Luke 22:42) tell us about our attitude when we pray for God's help?

22. *For personal reflection. Sharing optional.* Review your responses above (questions 18–21). Then speak to your Lord in prayer. (A helpful approach: Speak in words of adoration, telling Him how you praise Him for all that He is; confess your sins, your falling short of what He has called you to be; thank Him for all the blessings He has given you; ask Him for His help and guidance for the needs that are on your heart, the needs of your loved ones, and the needs of the hungry, persecuted, and people without Christ in this world.)

12. How do we *get the power* to grow in God-pleasing use of our money for our own and our neighbor's good? See 1 John 3:16–18, especially verse 16.

Day 4 • Read James 5:1–6

13. Compare James 1:9–11 with 5:1–6. What clue do you discover that James is addressing the *ungodly* rich in 5:1–6 and not rich Christians?

14. The phrase "last days" (James 5:3) occurs often in the Bible. See, for example, Isaiah 2:2; Acts 2:17; 2 Peter 3:3. After the *first* coming of the promised Savior, Jesus, only the *last* coming of Jesus and the end of the world lies ahead. What is our Lord's admonition to us Christians regarding these "last days" and *the* last day? See Matthew 25:13.

15. The fate of the wicked rich in the Day of Judgment is vividly pictured in the "rotted" clothes and money. To what horrible punishment does "eat your flesh like fire" (v. 3) refer? See Matthew 5:29–30.

Day 5 • Read James 5:1–6

16. James may well have been remembering Jesus' words in Matthew 6:20–21 when he wrote "you have hoarded wealth" (James 5:3). Thoughtfully and prayerfully read Jesus' words to you in Matthew 6:19–21. Think about your relationship to the people nearest to you—children, parents, friends. What *eternal* concerns do you have for them?

17. Summarize St. Paul's inspired commentary on storing up treasures in 1 Timothy 6:17–19. Which verse or concept in this text is most meaningful to you?

18. Another translation of James 5:6 is "you have killed the righteous man" (RSV). In what ways might this translation be a fitting description of Jesus? See Acts 7:52.

19. In what ways does that translation also fit with the persecuted Christians of that day—and today? See Acts 9:5.

9. a. According to verse 3, why are the prayers of many people not answered?

b. How and why *does* God answer prayer? See Matthew 7:7–11; 1 John 5:14.

Day 3 • Read James 4:4–6

10. In what sense were the people "adulterous" (v. 4)? See Jeremiah 3:20.

11. Friendship with the "world" and God are unalterably opposed, according to verse 4. What are some ungodly features of the world that are apparent today as we observe what is happening in our communities, read the daily newspaper, and hear TV accounts? (See also 1 John 2:15–17.)

12. Two translations of verse 5 are possible. In the first, "the spirit He caused to live in us" refers to God's creation of people (Genesis 2:7). Because of the fall, the human spirit "envies intensely," but God's grace (v. 6) is able to overcome human envy. Another possible translation capitalizes the word "Spirit"—the Holy Spirit "longs for" (envies) our full devotion. How does 1 Corinthians 6:19–20 fit with—and resolve—both translations? (See also Ephesians 4:30.)

Day 4 • Read James 4:7–10

13. Slowly and prayerfully read 1 Peter 5:8–9 and Ephesians 6:10–18, which describe the weapons God makes available to us to withstand the devil's attacks (James 4:7). Then sing or read "A Mighty Fortress Is Our God." What verse or verses speak most meaningfully to you?

14. What Old Testament priestly ritual does verse 8 point to? See Exodus 30:17–21 and Psalm 24:3–5.

15. What kind of "kill-joy" advice is this in verse 9? Isn't Christianity a religion of joy? See Luke 6:25b; 2 Corinthians 7:10; and Matthew 5:4.

16. How does Luke 18:9–14 illustrate verse 10?

Day 5 • Read James 4:11–12

17. In what way(s) does the judging of one's fellow believer in verse 11 differ from the judging mentioned in Galatians 6:1–5?

18. In what way(s) is the wrongful judging of verses 11 and 12 contrary to Jesus' words in Matthew 7:1–5, 12?

19. *For personal reflection. Sharing optional.* Think of people near and dear to you (in your family, workplace, congregation, etc.) and also some *not* so dear to you. In what specific ways have you fallen into judgmental words or behavior this past week or received wrongful judging from others? Speak to your heavenly Father, confessing your sin and leaning on His perfect love and forgiveness in Christ. Ask for the strengthening of His Spirit. Speak to the erring brother or sister as God counsels you in Galatians 6:1–5.

11. Give an example of this from daily life, even from your own experience.

12. In the examples that James gives, why is it so surprising that the tongue can wield such awesome influence?

13. Why does he use the image of fire to refer to the evil influence that the tongue often has?

Day 4 • Read James 3:7–8

14. a. Why do people tame all kinds of animals?

b. Is it easy to get any animal to do what you want instead of what it wants to do?

15. Why is it more difficult to tame the tongue than to train even a wild animal? See Romans 7:21–25.

16. In what sense is it true that no one can tame the tongue?

17. What is the "restless evil," the "deadly poison" mentioned in verse 8? See Psalm 58:3–4; Matthew 23:29, 33; John 8:44.

Day 5 • Read James 3:9–12

18. a. What are the two kind of words that come out of our mouths?

b. In what ways are they different?

19. How do James's readers, including we ourselves, sometimes tend to feel about this?

20. How does James comment on this attitude?

21. How are others affected when someone who praises God also curses people?

12. What is lacking in the "faith" referred to in verse 19?

Day 4 • Read James 2:20–24; Genesis 22:1–19; Hebrews 11:17–19

13. a. What came first in Abraham, his faith or his obedience?

b. Which was cause and which was effect?

14. What does James say caused God to credit Abraham as righteous (v. 23), that is, to declare that everything was right between them?

15. The Scripture quoted in this connection is Genesis 15:6. When did this happen in relation to the events of Genesis 22:1–19?

16. a. How does Hebrews 11:17–19 explain Abraham's obedience?

b. How do these verses help us to properly understand verse 21?

Day 5 • Read James 2:25–26; Hebrews 11:31; Joshua 2:1–21

17. According to the account in Joshua 2, what caused Rahab to respond as she did to the God of Israel and His people?

18. How does Hebrews 11:31 explain Rahab's action?

19. a. Does anything in either passage approve of her way of life?

b. Does God's dealing with Rahab remind you of anything similar in Jesus' ministry? See, for example, Matthew 21:31 and John 8:1–11.

20. **Challenge question.** Reflect on verse 26 and develop a brief story illustration that will illustrate what James is saying here about the importance of good works in the Christian life. Understand "spirit" as "signs of life."

b. How should we react to what the mirror of the Law reveals about us?

c. How do 2:9–11 expand on this point?

11. When we hear what God's Word says about our sinfulness and repent, we are ready to hear something even more important that God wants to say to us. James refers to it as "the perfect law that gives freedom" (v. 25). This is different from the Law that exposes and condemns our sins.

a. What do we usually call this part of God's Word? See Romans 1:16.

b. What does it do for us? See Romans 1:16 and 8:1–4.

c. How does Paul refer to this part of God's Word in Romans 8:2?

12. When he speaks about someone who is "religious," James means someone who has heard and believed God's Word and is responding to it in life. What two changes in such a person are described in verse 27?

Day 4 • Read James 2:1–9; Luke 6:20–26

13. a. Are the rich and poor people mentioned in James 2:1–9 Christians?

b. On what do you base your answer?

14. Under what circumstances might we or our congregation show the kind of partiality described here?

15. Why should we not favor the rich or be overly impressed by them (see vv. 6–7)?

16. What special favor does God often show the poor (2:5)?

Day 5 • Read James 2:12–13; Romans 8:1; Matthew 25:31–46

17. In James 2:12–13 who are those who have the "law that gives freedom" (the Gospel)?

18. Why are they expected to show mercy to others?

19. a. Is God merciful to us only if we first show mercy to others?

b. How can we lose God's mercy?

c. What does it show when we forgive—or refuse to forgive—others? See Ephesians 4:32.

20. What is the nature of the judgment that they will experience? See Romans 8:1 and Matthew 25:31–46.

Romans 5:1–5

2 Corinthians 1:3–7; 12:7–10

Philippians 1:27–30

Day 3 • Read James 1:6; Matthew 14:22–34

9. When asking God for wisdom or anything else, we must "believe and not doubt" (v. 6). To a suffering or persecuted Christian what would be some aspects of that faith?

10. What would be some aspects of the doubt that we might have at a time of great trouble in our lives? (If you are willing, share any personal experiences you've had with doubts in a time of great trial in your life.)

11. Because of our continuing sinfulness we often experience doubt and faith at the same time. Consider Peter's experience (Matthew 14:22–34). What gave him the faith to step out on the water?

12. a. What caused him to doubt, and what were the consequences?

b. How did Jesus respond to Peter when he wavered?

c. How did Peter respond to Jesus' rescue?

d. What might we learn from this?

Day 4 • Read James 1:9–12

13. Jesus turns things upside down. He makes the poor rich and the rich poor. How can you tell that Christians and not unbelievers are addressed in these verses?

14. How does God make the poor rich? See Luke 1:53; 6:20; 1 Peter 5:6.

15. How does God make the rich poor (vv. 10–12)? See also Luke 6:24 and 12:13–21.

16. What special temptations are faced by the poor and by the rich?

Day 5 • Read James 1:13–18

17. *Temptation* and *trial* are the same word in Greek, the language in which this letter was originally written. How are trials (difficulties from outside ourselves) and temptations (to sin) similar?

18. a. How can trials become temptations?

b. Why can't it be said that temptations are also trials?

19. a. What is the superlative "good and perfect gift" (v. 17)? See John 3:13–18.

b. How does that gift assure us about other important gifts that we need (e.g., wisdom to deal with trials and temptations)? See Romans 8:31–32.

20. It is important to "nip in the bud" every sinful inclination.

a. How does James explain the reason for this in verse 15? We tend to excuse ourselves for sinning (I can't help it!).

b. How does James speak to that attitude (vv. 13–14)?